SIMPLE SCIENCE FUN

Experiences with
Light, Sound, Air and Water

by Bob Ridiman

A Humpty Dumpty Book

Parents' Magazine Press / New York

Text and illustrations Copyright © 1972 by Bob Ridiman
All rights reserved
Printed in the United States of America

Library of Congress Cataloging in Publication Data
Ridiman, Bob.
  Simple science fun.

  SUMMARY: Simple experiments reveal the principles
of light, sound, air, and water.
    1. Science—Experiments—Juvenile literature.
[1. Science—Experiments] I. Title.
PZ10.R443Si   530'.028   72-664
ISBN 0-8193-0607-X
ISBN 0-8193-0606-1 (lib. bdg.)

LIGHT

SOUND

AIR

WATER

LIGHT

THE SUN
is about
this much
bigger than
THE EARTH.

Most of our light comes from the sun.

The sun gives us day and night.

You can see why the sun gives us day and night.

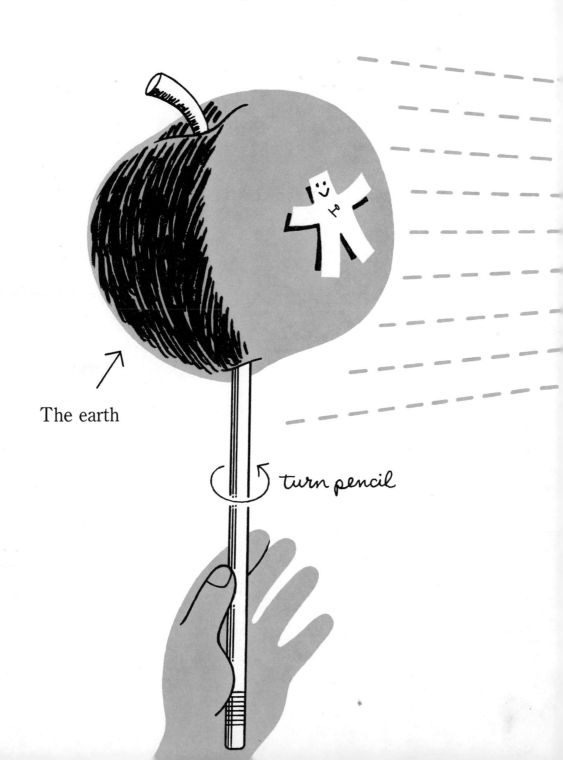

The earth

turn pencil

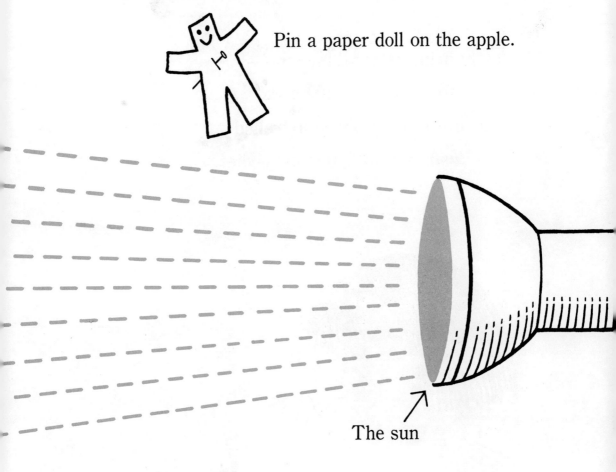

Pin a paper doll on the apple.

The sun

In a dark room turn, or *revolve,*

the apple. Watch the paper doll go

from day to night and back to day.

The earth makes a complete *revolution* every
24 hours giving us one day and one night.

Light helps us see things.
We see things that make
their own light. They are called
luminous (LOO-mi-nus) bodies.

The stars

A campfire

We also see things
that *do not* make
their own light.

A puppy

A doll

We see them because they
reflect, or bounce back, light
from luminous bodies.

Which one of these

is *not* a luminous body?

Sun

Moon

neon

Electric sign

Fireflies

Lantern

Answer:

The moon is not a luminous body because
its light is reflected from the sun.

16

Sunlight shining
through raindrops
makes all the colors
of the rainbow.

Here's how
you can make a
RAINBOW.

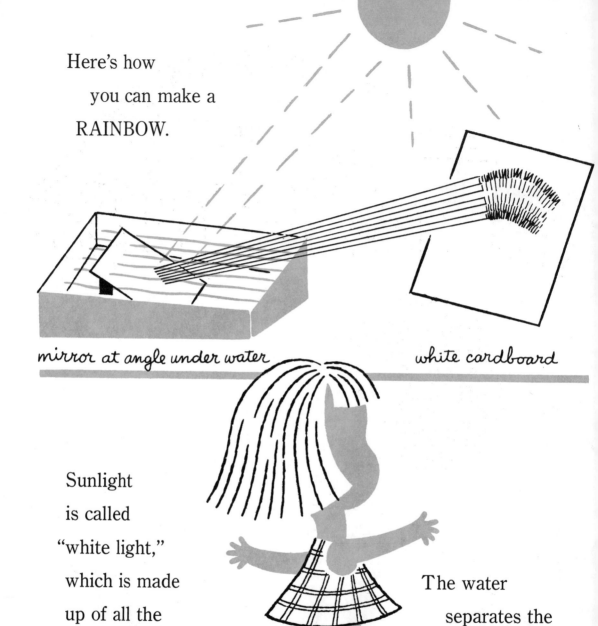

mirror at angle under water   white cardboard

Sunlight
is called
"white light,"
which is made
up of all the
colors of
the rainbow.

The water
separates the
colors in the
"white light."

18

Copy on
cardboard
and color.
Push a
pin through
the center.

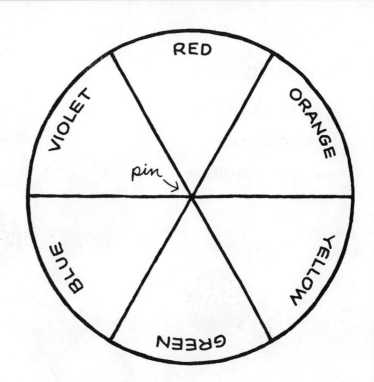

RAINBOW COLOR WHEEL

Spin the wheel
faster and faster
until all
the colors
blend together
and look white.

An *optical illusion*
is something that
looks different
from what it really is.

Does one flower
have a larger
center than the
other flower?

20

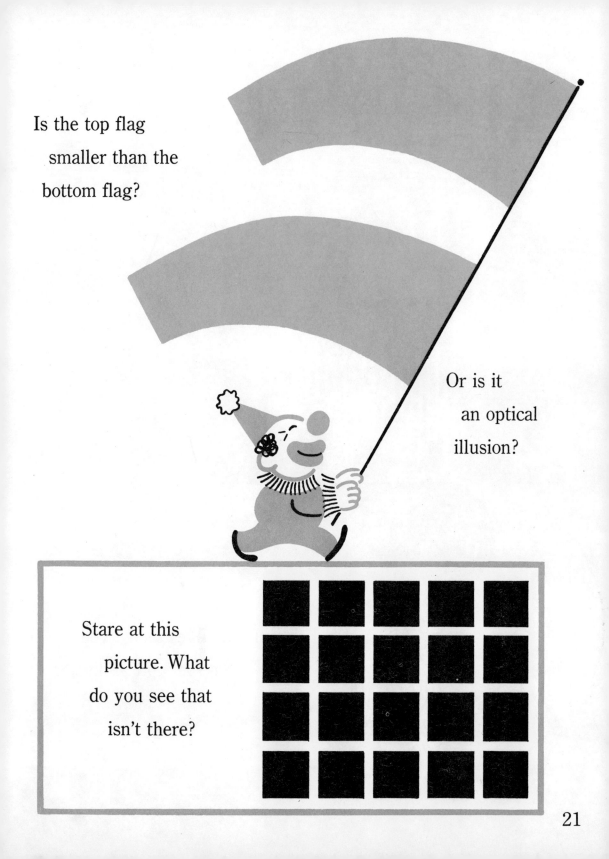

Is the top flag
smaller than the
bottom flag?

Or is it
an optical
illusion?

Stare at this
picture. What
do you see that
isn't there?

Is Henry's
high hat higher
than it is wide?

If your eyes fooled you
it's an optical illusion.

SOUND

You can feel your
vocal cords *vibrate*
when you talk.

Sounds are made
when something
vibrates, or moves back
and forth very fast.

Hold a thin ruler on
a table. Push down on
the end, then let go.

Listen to the
vibrations.

Press a thin strip of paper
or a blade of grass
between your thumbs.
Blow hard to make it
vibrate and make sounds.

Guitar strings
vibrate and make
musical sounds.

rubber bands of same length
but different thickness

You can *see* the vibrations
when you pluck this
CAKE PAN GUITAR.

Tap an empty glass.

The glass vibrates
too fast for you to see.
But you can *hear* the
vibrations make a *high* sound.

Tap a glass full of water.
The glass vibrates slower
and makes a *low* sound.

LOW   HIGH

You can make an

8-NOTE XYLOPHONE

by using a different amount

of water in each glass.

DO   RE   MI   FA   SO   LA   TI   DO

Other musical instruments you can make.

COFFEE CAN DRUM

rubber from balloon
stretched tight

rubber
band

COFFEE
2 lbs.

POT LID CYMBALS

Most of the sounds you hear
travel through the air.

Sound vibrations travel better through
solid things than through the air.

Indians could hear
far-away hoofbeats
through the ground.

Listen to a clock ticking.
Then listen to the sound
of the ticking as it
travels through
a wooden table.

Sound travels through string in these

SILVERWARE CHIMES.

Tie silverware close together in the center of a 3-foot string. Hold the ends of the string in your ears with your fingertips.

Make your own TELEPHONE.

punch holes in 2 empty cans

knot

long string →
← stretched tight

knot

The sound of your voice
travels through the string
to your friend's ear.

AIR

You can't *see* air but you can *feel* air.

You can feel *hot* air.

You can feel *cold* air.

You can feel *moving* air.

When air is heated it *expands*,

or takes up more space.

You can see this happen.

balloon

ice cold
empty
bottle

hot water

What happens when
the air in the bottle is
expanded by the heat?

Moving air is wind.

You can see the wind
spin your pinwheel.

Copy this pattern to make your PINWHEEL.

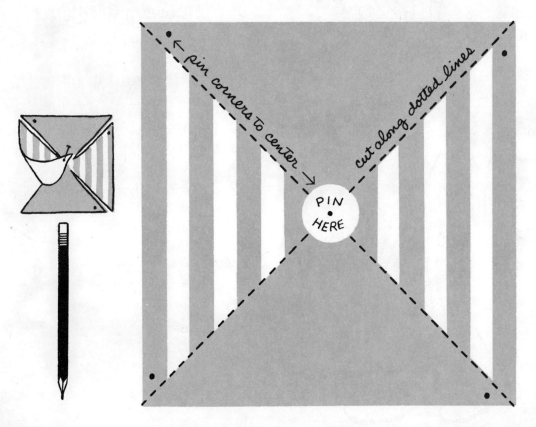

pin corners to center

cut along dotted lines

PIN
HERE

Air pushes in *all* directions. You can prove it!

Cover a full glass of water with a thin card. Hold card in place and quickly turn glass upside down.

(*Do this trick over the sink.*)

Now let go of the card.

Air pushes *up*
against the card and keeps
the water in the glass.

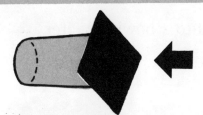

Does air push *sideways*?

Air pushes *down*. Try to
blow the card off the glass.

Air pushes in *all* directions.

Air can make water run uphill

with this plastic flex-straw *siphon* (SI-fun).

Fill the straw with water.
Keep water in straw with
fingers over ends. Put short
end of straw into a bowl of water.
Then take fingers from ends.

keep straw bent ⇘

Air pushes *down* on water
in bowl and forces water *up*
into straw, over top of bowl.

WATER

There is as much water
in the world today as
when dinosaurs lived.

Water

is

never

lost!

45

Water is used over and over again in
NATURE'S WATER CYCLE.

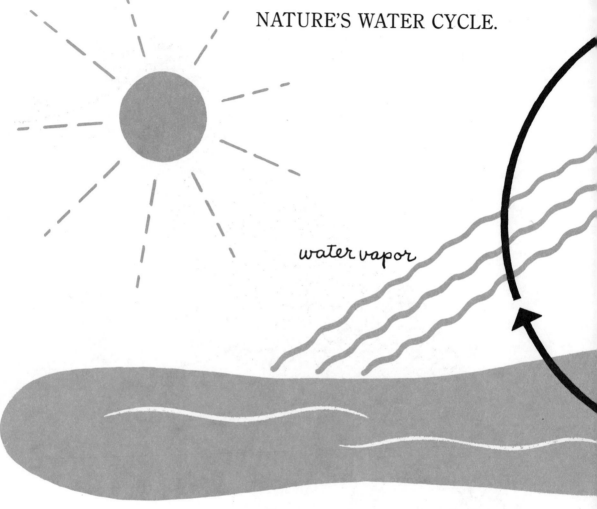

water vapor

The heat of the sun changes the earth's
LIQUID water into water VAPOR. When water
vapor cools, it changes back into liquid water.

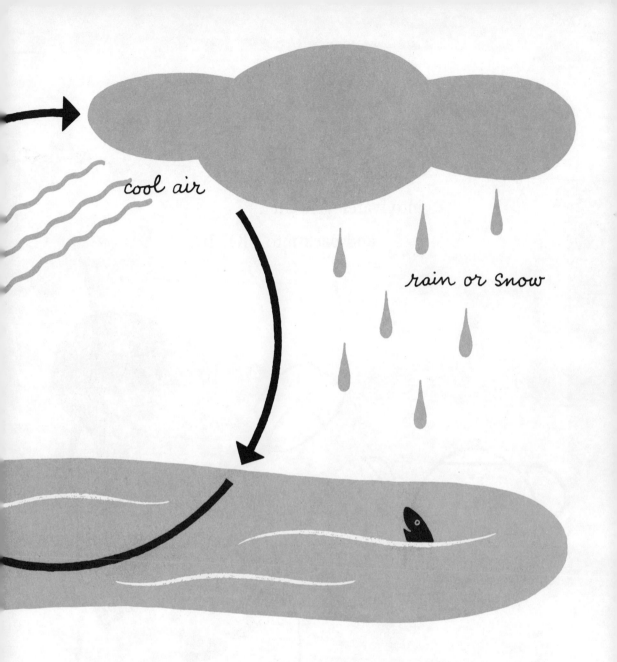

cool air

rain or snow

These changes are called the *water cycle*
because they happen over and over again.
Water is never lost—it is *recycled.*

Make your own water cycle.

Change LIQUID water

into water VAPOR

and back into LIQUID.

When LIQUID water freezes
it becomes a SOLID called *ice*.

Ice protects living things
in frozen lakes and rivers.

High in the mountains are
man-made lakes called
reservoirs (REZ-er-vwars).

Water travels DOWN
from the reservoir,
then flows UP
into our houses.

50

Water seeks its own level. Water flows UP
as high as the place from which it started.

Pour water into the
reservoir, a cupful at a
time. How high does the
water rise in the house
after each cupful?

BOB RIDIMAN was born in Elmira, New York and grew up in Cincinnati, Ohio where he graduated from the Ohio Mechanics Institute. After a number of years working in advertising as an artist and art director, he now works as a freelance artist, painter and silversmith. He has contributed many simple, clearly illustrated science activities to *Humpty Dumpty's Magazine* and other children's publications. Mr. Ridiman and his wife make their home in Aroya Seca, New Mexico.